"The" Game

Recollections and Reflections of a Teen Coming of Age in a Small Midwestern Town

C. Gamble

"The" Game – Recollections and Reflections of a Teen Coming of Age in a Small Midwestern Town

Copyright © 2024 by Charles Gamble

All Rights Reserved

No part of this book may be reproduced or transmitted in any form or by any means, electronic or mechanical, including photocopying, recording, or by any information storage and retrieval system without the written permission of the author, except where permitted by law.

This manuscript is dedicated to the memory of Rich, classmate and friend.

Preface

The author is a 1967 graduate of Edgerton (Wisconsin) High School. He was not born and raised in the small town of Edgerton, population 4,000. In fact, he was only a student there for two brief years (junior and senior). But that is precisely the point. Edgerton – the town, the school, the teachers, and most of all, his friends, made an indelible mark on his nostalgic soul.

The author, now a septuagenarian, harbors and recalls some of his fondest memories through the prism of an adolescent preparing for adulthood. Thus, this essay marks an attempt, a Pulitzer it's not, to recount and share those two short years with the reader. Trite, corny—say what you want. It is simply an unabashed sentimental journey. And, in doing so, the author thanks his teachers, friends, and classmates for being a part of his life when it was most needed. More on that later.

Gratefully, the author has been able to stay in touch with each and every one of his closest high school friends, lifelong friends.

Thank you, guys. Hope you enjoy the read.

Seems like yesterday but it was long ago… Bob Seger

"The" Game – Recollections and Reflections of a Teen Coming of Age in a Small Midwestern Town

It was the teen's third high school in three years. From Williams Bay (on Lake Geneva) to Green Bay, to Edgerton he journeyed. The Summer of 1965 was commencing when the moving van arrived at the prescribed destination – a two-story farmhouse on the outskirts of a place the teen had never been. His new residence was aged, appearing at first blush to be of Victorian vintage. The spacious front yard was occupied by huge veteran oak trees bordered by a massive, whitewashed building, in short, an old dairy barn. Additional weathered structures were adjacent to the garage and backyard. The residents of this new home were not limited to mom, dad, kids, and Spike the Labrador. The teen immediately noticed a committee of livestock prowling the adjoining pasture. These occupants constituted a gathering of Black Angus cattle the teen would quickly learn possessed a collective attitude– downright ornery.

All of this was quite a change from Green Bay where the teen lived just three blocks from Lambeau Field, then called City Stadium. The marked venue change from city to country was no issue with the teen. Moving to a country setting felt like slipping on a pair of well-worn, comfortable slippers.

In spite of the teen's positive initial impression, it didn't take long for that familiar feeling to take hold. Once again, he was beginning a summer without a friend in sight and would start the new school year assuming the role of "the new kid". His sophomore year was now history and he would have to occupy himself until commencing his junior year. Friends or not, he soon learned of the proximity of the farmhouse to the nearby Rock River - within walking distance. Over the course of the teen's stay in Edgerton, he would log countless hours sitting on the bank of the Rock River.

A river seems like a magic thing. A magic, moving, living part of the very earth itself—Laura Gilpin

A day or two passed and it was time for the teenager to find his bearings. The farmhouse was just outside the official city limits, but downtown Edgerton was easily within walking distance. It was just a matter of walking down River Road to the junction of Highway 59 where downtown could be reached in half an hour, give or take. Now having nothing but time on his hands, coupled with favorable weather, the teen took his inaugural walk to downtown Edgerton. Down the prescribed route he went, eventually encountering what was obviously "the main drag". Starting from the intersection of Fulton and Main, the downtown featured multiple businesses that required exploration.

The teen noticed a variety of typical small-town retailers. While the north side of Fulton Street represented the heart of the business district, the south side was a decided contrast. The south side of Fulton St. was dominated by the Chicago Northwestern Railroad and a host of large white brick buildings, which were part and parcel of the lifeblood of Edgerton and the surrounding area – tobacco. Sure enough, tobacco grows in Edgerton, Wisconsin! As the teen would eventually glean from local history, Edgerton and northern Rock County provided a substantial percentage of cigar wrappings to complement their cousin industries on the East

Coast. The white, chalky buildings, warehouses, and loading docks created a "skyline" of sorts. For a teen, there was not a whole lot of interest there, so he explored the stores and businesses on the north side of Fulton Street.

The teen had yet to travel a block from Fulton and Main when he discovered what would be his most frequented shop in town – the Coast-to-Coast Hardware Store. What a find! Aside from the usual array of hardware items, there was a sporting goods section – right up the teen's alley. Having brought his prized possession from Williams Bay (his going away present from his pal Mike) via Green Bay his single-shot Springfield .22 rifle, he found a convenient place to resupply his ammunition needs. Not only did this establishment show ample dedication to the world of hunting, the collection of fishing tackle was equally impressive. As far as the nimrod was concerned, this place had just about everything he would require.

Moving along and continuing down Fulton, the teen passed several bars. They had names like The Office, Rollie's Roost, and The Oats Bin. As it was summer, and a warm day at that, he could easily discern when he was approaching one of the drinking establishments. The aroma, if you will, was a dead giveaway as the propped-open doors provided necessary ventilation on that warm and humid day.

Further on he recognized the pool hall, just next to the cigar store. The teen peered in the front window and could see a few pool enthusiasts as well as a small gathering of old timers occupying a card table in the rear area. As the teen continued to pan the room from a distance, he recalled his father's edict – "I don't want to see you in that place (pool hall)." The teen wasn't sure what that was all about, but he was generally not inclined to challenge the former Marine's mandates – like it or not. But …. He was a card-carrying teenager now. The usually compliant offspring was loathe to get into trouble with "Big Man" (his sis' term for dad). In spite of his father's moratorium on crossing the threshold of this ostensible den of inequity, he did, on occasion, enter cautiously, always with a chum as a second pair of eyes. Besides, how could anyone expect a teenager to resist a glass of coke that only fetched a nickel? Yup – a nickel, which in turn, afforded the teen a glazed donut to go with.

Past the pool hall was another watering hole. Then, the teen was besieged by an unmistakable aroma – fresh bread and baked goods. No mistaking, it was the town bakery. As is customary, the hard-to-resist goods were prominently displayed in the front window – for all to see while daring the pedestrians to simply pass by as if unaware. Unbeknownst, the teen would later acquire employment at the bakery, compliments of help from his bud Dick (aka Rich).

The teen was running out of real estate. His points of interest were petering out but he felt quite satisfied with his cursory view of town. Approaching the end of the block he encountered a small corner grocery store and, of course, another tavern. So, it was time to retrace his steps and head home, his new home. The ascent to the farmhouse was initiated. Once past the retailers, his curiosity was piqued. Having crossed the Fulton and Main St. intersection, it was a short distance to his dad's new place of employment – The Highway Trailer factory. Little did he know, Highway Trailer would provide the youth with summer employment and fund his expenses for his sophomore year at the University of Wisconsin.

For his next two years in Edgerton, the teen would make the trip to town and back many times, the majority of which were on foot. During his senior year, he frequently made the trip to town, dribbling a basketball, as per his coach's edict. From River Road down Hwy 59 down and back he went rain or shine (uphill both ways of course).

As it turned out, that Summer of 1965 was relatively uneventful, downright dull at times. The newcomer had yet to start school, so the paucity of friends required him to improvise if he was going to get through the Summer. It was either walking to town (been there and done that) or gathering his fishing tackle and heading to the river, the Rock River. The river usually won out. Didn't take long – the teen became very fond of his treks to what would become his personal fishing hole. Out the back door with fishing gear in tow, he had to pass by a small barn that usually housed a dozen or so ill-tempered, territorial Black Angus cows. Once safely past the four-legged landlords he traversed the first leg of his journey, an open pasture, always keeping an eye on his bovine chums while they kept an eye on him. Quite hilly it was until he reached the adjacent alfalfa field and, what should have been a benign leg on his way to the river, became an unexpected obstacle course. Upon entering the knee-high dew-covered vegetation, out came a squadron of red-winged blackbirds. Not happy with the intruder, the airborne aggressors served notice the teen was an unwelcomed guest. It wasn't quite like a scene from Alfred Hitchcock's "The Birds," but, at the very least, the teen felt like he was walking through a golf course driving range without a helmet.

Finally reaching the end of the cultivated field and excising himself from being an unwanted visitor, his destination was in sight. The lazy summer current of the Rock River could be gleaned through a grove of mature oak trees. Working his way down the hill toward the river, he found an opening in the brush. Standing under a large burr oak tree that was hugging the bank, he found the perfect spot to ply his trade. After being bombarded by the blackbirds, with his jeans and tennis shoes soaked from the morning dew, he could sit and relax (and dry out).

The Rock River represented quite a contrast from his old fishing hole, the Williams Bay town pier on Lake Geneva. Nonetheless, to the avid fisherman, there is no such thing as a bad day when you have a fishing pole in hand. As the teen would soon learn, the river was not as populated with the spiny rays he was accustomed to pursuing. But – fishing is fishing, and the teen was just glad to be in the countryside again.

Time to wet a line. Not really knowing what he was fishing for – just fish, he hooked a weighty one right off the bat. His prize was carefully coaxed to the bank. Upon further inspection, the nimrod had no idea what he had caught. Nothing like anything he had seen before. It was a peculiar looking specimen with large opaque eyes. He was later told by a passerby it was a walleye – a very propitious start for his first outing on the Rock River.

The teen fell in love with the river as if it were his first girlfriend. The river was never angry or extreme – always a rhythmic, melodic pulse. Watching the gentle, sinuous current, with its subtle variations, was mesmerizing. Over time, the river would serve as a place of respite and recreation whenever he and a chum or two wanted to enjoy the outdoors. Sometimes after completing a day of fishing, the teen and his chum(s) would roll out the sleeping bags, gaze at the stars, and ponder life and the future. Boy! What a way to live.

With the Summer of '65 in the books, it was time for the teen to prepare for the day he was all too familiar with – the first day of school - another new school. In fact, Edgerton represented his third high school in three years. Redundantly, he was "that new kid."

With his junior year class schedule in hand, he navigated the building's geography with rapt attention. The last thing the teen wanted was a tardy slip on his inaugural voyage. The neophyte found the physical plant to be quite user-friendly. All in all, the first day was a success – made it to all classes on time. His customary anxiety had abated some, but he still felt alone amongst a crowd.

It takes courage to grow up and become who you really are - E.E. Cummings.

The first week was generating a greater sense of comfort with each passing day with one unexpected, fortuitous event. By the luck of the draw, the teen was seated next to a personable fellow who initiated a conversation. It was in Mr. Greene's psychology class that he met his new chum, a friend who would become a lifer. Terry was his name. The two guys found several things in common – sports, for one, provided ample common ground. It didn't take long for the two to become better acquainted. Aside from class, the teens found themselves playing two hand touch football games on a fairly regular basis - sometimes at Terry's, in his backyard off Hwy 51, or at the teen's on River Road.

Education is not preparation for life; education is life itself—John Dewey.
Photo by Dennis Balch

So, the teen was easing into his junior year at Edgerton Community High School. There was one thing the teen appreciated about his introduction to his new school that was all too plain. Where his sophomore year in Green Bay, at an all-boys parochial school, was a dud on all accounts, the new social milieu was more than a welcomed change – GIRLS. All shapes and sizes: blonde, brunettes, redheads. So many pretty girls. Although the teen was a card-carrying introvert, and never having mustered the courage to ask a female out on a date, he was nonetheless subject to being periodically smitten.

The teen's first semester of his junior year was proceeding uneventfully. Deeper into the Fall of 1965, the teen was alerted to the up-and-coming basketball tryouts. Basketball was not his first love, but with a modest interest and some ability, he thought he would give it a try. The varsity was stacked with talent that year, leaving him no room on that roster. Thus, the undersized teen was assigned to the junior varsity, coached by Mr. Repka. The JV squad included two fellow juniors, Gary and Joe. Both would become lifelong friends. In fact, Joe and Gary have made a point of keeping in touch some sixty years later.

J.V. BASKETBALL TOP ROW: Coach Repka, J. Boabon, B. Richardson, G. Purnell, L. Miller, J. Peterson, A. Kjernes, D. Balch, M. McGinnity, D. Johnson. BOTTOM ROW: C. Gamble, R. Gorde, C. Johnson, D. Bilborn, S. Shower, S. Maves, J. Oran.

The first semester came and went. The teen was already halfway through his junior year of high school. The JV basketball season was nearing completion. No girlfriend yet but plenty of heartthrobs – if they only knew. Spring was finally nudging Winter out of the way. The adjacent farm fields were showing signs of waking up as the snow was slowly receding. It seemed like a long, cold winter but probably no different than most – just a typical Wisconsin Winter.

Now midway through his second semester, the teen had a decision to make. Sports were always on his "to-do" list, but which one? Baseball was always his first love since he learned how to swing a Louisville Slugger. But, he hadn't played "hardball" since lettering his freshman year in Williams Bay. Track or baseball? The decision became easier when he learned his new buds Terry, Rollie, Joe, and Gary all signed up for track. Track it was. Although he didn't regret his decision, not much came of it. That prized varsity letter was yet to see the front of a maroon letterman's jacket.

Track had concluded and final exams were navigated successfully – just Summer ahead. This time, however, there was a conspicuous absence of the usual moving van at the front door. The teen realized readily he was finishing high school at a place that was growing on him. It was starting to feel like home.

The Summer of 1966 was unique; no boxes to pack, no moving van showed up as it had in the two previous summers. Not since eighth grade, the teen could continue with his same group of friends without the dreadful goodbyes. How novel – he had friends and could plan activities, not something he was at all used to. The river was a popular destination for fishing and light camping. Rollie's was just down the road on Hwy 59. Just a hop, skip, and a jump the teen could be at Rollie's conjuring up some athletic competition. In short, he got to see his pals often – a welcomed change from past Summers.

The teen, not unlike others his age, required funds to support a number of his prized activities. With the help of his new friend Dick (aka Rich), he managed to get a part-time job at the bakery. It was nice to have some cash in his pocket for a change (no pun intended). His first job was nothing special and certainly not a career move but the teen could at least finance his rabbit and squirrel hunting outings.

The bakery job, being just part-time, allowed him time to make a few extra bucks with other endeavors. One of the teen's classmate's dads owned the local Texaco Station on Main St. In addition to the usual services, he owned a pump truck, a septic pump truck, to be specific. As it worked out, his chum Dennis asked him to help out on occasion. What else? Pumping out septic tanks and distributing the proceeds to a nearby farm field. The teen was not necessarily proud, but he believed his chum deliberately drove the "Honey Dipper" through downtown Edgerton just to embarrass him, more like irritate him. The teen was supposed to receive compensation for his efforts. That was all well and good, but he never warmed up to the idea of being seen in town, occupying the passenger seat of the Honey Dipper. At the very least, the two jobs provided sufficient funds for his ammunition needs and other miscellaneous expenses.

Just prior to the Summer of 1966, the teen passed his driver's test (second try), which afforded him occasional use of the family vehicle – a lime green Rambler station wagon. Periodically, the teen's father (Big Man) would ask if the teen wanted to borrow said vehicle on a Friday or Saturday night. What's the saying? "Beggars can't be choosers." The teen usually preferred one of his chums, Joe, Rollie, or Ron, to stop by and pick him up. There was just something about driving through town in a lime green Rambler station wagon. Necessity being the mother of invention, the teen occasionally took his dad up on the offer.

The Summer of '66 was one of the best on record, at least in the last two years. The teen was certainly acclimating to his new home and new friends. Work, friends, and recreation encapsulated the teen's summer days. Trips to the river were frequent and walks to Rollie's were eagerly anticipated. Even those long summer days that were eventually punctuated by darkness, the teen would make his way back home from Rollie's "gym" compliments of Hwy 59. No one really knew how late it was, but the end of each basketball game was usually decided by fatigue more than anything else. Sometimes it was so dark journeying back home the teen could barely see his hand in front of his face.

So, Rollie's barn became a special gathering place. Having negotiated the woods and hills – not forget those onery Black Angus, the teen would eventually reach the highway and shortly thereafter, Rollie's red brick farmhouse was visible. Game on – never knew who would show up for the game of the week but sides were quickly chosen. The loft in the barn hadn't been used for years, so it was logical basketball hoops should be staged at both ends. The curvature of the old tin roof accommodated eight- or nine-foot baskets. The old floor was generally stable but tin flashing had to be tacked down when one of the competitors, say, a heavy-footed one, broke through the weathered flooring – like his pal Joe (6'-5" and 235 lbs.). On one particular occasion, Joe broke through the "gym" floor and the assembled teammates had to go to the lower level and retrieve his size 12's. Repairs were made, and the competition continued into the late hours of the evening.

For the most part, these contests of skill (and stamina) were conducted on a friendly basis. There was one occasion when adolescent tempers were pushed to the limit. Rollie's younger brother Dale was a frequent participant in those battles of pride. Dale was two- or three years Rollie's junior and could flare up from time to time. The basketball game was moving along without incident until Dale got his hackles up, having been fouled. Frustrated to the brink, Dale grabbed the basketball, and with considerable velocity, threw it straight up in the air. A body in motion tends to stay in motion. Not in Rollie's gym. The old tin roof with all those protruding galvanized nails conspired to deflate the only basketball the youths had. So that particular contest was unceremoniously brought to a conclusion. Fortunately, that type of incident was an anomaly as the games usually concluded with something like – "Thanks guys, see you later or see you guys in school."

The teen spent countless hours at Rollie's, always feeling welcomed by Rollie and his family. Those folks were simply the proverbial "salt of the earth." Rollie came from good stock, always welcoming and unpretentious – a friend for life.

Senior Year

The 16 year-old was now on the threshold of leaving the nest. Thankfully, the teen's family stayed put, allowing the youth to finish his schooling in Edgerton – a welcome relief. No longer feeling like the new kid, he could navigate his senior year in a normal fashion, sorta. What are you going to do after you graduate? Where are you going to college? To complicate decisions about life after high school, there was a war going on. Questions and answers would be sorted out over the course of the year, but the teen still had two semesters left.

The Teachers

Over the course of his two-year enrollment, the teen was mentored by a special and outstanding crop of high school teachers. So, any nostalgic discussion of attending Edgerton Community High School mandates recognizing the "foot soldiers".

"I don't like that teacher" was never in the teen's vocabulary. Having no specific criteria regarding the skill level of any of his teachers, the teen just knew he was in good hands. It was simply visceral. Maybe it was just luck of the draw, but the teen trusted and respected the entire lot – no exceptions. His teachers, unassigned or unwittingly, often served as "guidance counselors."

Here is a brief journey back to the classroom to support his thesis that Edgerton High was gifted with a talented group of educators.

There was Mr. Greene. Having an interest (ultimately a career path) in psychology, dating back to junior high days, the teen signed up for Mr. Greene's psychology class. Day one was pretty typical – passing out textbooks and assigning seating. This is where the nervous new kid would be introduced to a lifelong friend. Terry was a short, bespectacled fellow. It was generally the case the introverted teenager waited for the other guy to initiate conversation. Terry did just that – asking where the teen came from and so forth. From that point on, the two would converse, especially about sports, and enjoy playing basketball and organizing two-hand touch football contests.

As the assigned seats were all doled out, the teen noticed he was assigned a pretty blonde girl as a neighbor. It didn't take the teen long to figure out his new classmate was outgoing, to say the least, more accurately - loquacious.

Back to Mr. Greene. Mr. Greene was an imposing figure – probably played offensive line on a football team, the teen surmised. His new psych teacher had dark black hair and sported a flat top, quite common back in the day. Always wearing a white dress shirt, without fail, Mr. Greene complimented his wardrobe with a skinny black tie that looked more like a belt than a tie. At first blush, Mr. Greene's outward appearance suggested he had a beer and bowl of nails for breakfast. As the saying goes, "appearances can be deceptive." In spite of his imposing physical presence, Mr. Greene was no match for the teen's neighbor Sandy. Once, he became annoyed with the talkative young lady and barked out – "Sandra, shut up! Stop talking." Not intimidated whatsoever, Sandra barked back – "I wasn't talking to you!" That was quintessential Mr. Greene – tough football coach but no match for a diminutive teenage female.

No one loved or conveyed the love of the subject matter more than Mr. Ruscyck. History was his expertise as well as his passion. Mr. R always sported a colorful tie, madras it was called back in the '60s. "History is so boring" – not so fast. Whenever Mr. R. wanted to emphasize a point, he would morph into a Shakespearean character reenacting a historical event. Armed with his "bible"- U.S. history authored by Todd and Curti (Dr. Curti having taught at the University of Wisconsin), Mr. R. could quote chapter and verse about the Frederick Jackson Turner thesis. Simply, Mr. R. was dedicated to his craft and his students. Even for the most disinterested student, Mr. R.'s enthusiasm was infectious.

Mr. Bauer was the teen's physics teacher. Although Mr. B. gave the teen a well-deserved, hard-earned at that, final semester C grade, the student respected Mr. B.'s dedication to his profession. Mr. B.'s enthusiasm for teaching was palpable. Mr. B. would have easily been mistaken for a NASA engineer as his teaching attire was as predictable as sunrise and sunset. His salt and pepper crewcut complimented his white short-sleeved shirt with a pocket protector, stuffed with ballpoint pens and mechanical pencils. Rain or shine, 80 degrees or 20 below zero, Mr. Bauer always wore the same uniform. Mr. B. would best be described as a demanding teacher but never unfair. The C grade the teen "earned" didn't come close to describing what Mr. B. had taught him that semester.

Mr. Steffan was your "typical" P.E. teacher, in appearance. His physique and mannerisms mimicked that of a bouncer employed at an Irish Pub. He was short, stocky, sporting arms like Popeye. With a haircut to match, it was obvious his trips to the barber's chair were rarely required. Mr. S.'s P.E. classes included an array of sporting activities or units, as they were called. Mr. S. could be as demanding as the next teacher, but it was obvious he had a soft spot for those less athletically gifted. Conversely, the star athletes best not think they were going to coast through Mr. S.'s P.E. class. And, one thing that stood out, at least in the teen's mind's eye, was Mr. S.'s vigilance. He was not your stereotypical "jock". Mr. S. seemed to know everything happening in Edgerton High School.

It was late in the teen's senior year. While doing warm-ups, more precisely pushups, Mr. S. announced to the class, "Charlie's got a girlfriend." Surprised and equally embarrassed, the teen could not figure out how Mr. S. came up with that. True or not (it was true), the teen privately appreciated the attention. Mr. S. cared about his students.

No discussion of the teen's Edgerton teachers would be complete without crediting Mrs. Pavlik. Mrs. Pavlik knew her stuff. Assigned to Mrs. P.'s college prep literature class, the teen quickly surmised, "She's a real pro". Mrs. P. was a diminutive woman with shoulder length dark hair. Mrs. P.'s syllabus appeared onerous but manageable. Any malingering or dawdling could be costly. It was a hard but valuable lesson learned by the teen and some of his colleagues right out of the gate (in other words – first quarter grades). The teen and a handful of his getting-ready-for-college buddies received a grade of D. It wasn't a typo. Yup – the future of America was called into question. Mrs. P. was not fooling around. What she expected from the aspiring was not delivered and she served notice forthwith. Needless to say, the proverbial ship (2nd quarter grades) was righted and the teen and his pals responded as they should have from the very outset. Thank you, Mrs. P.!

Senior High School Semester Honor Roll

Seniors; 3.5 or above; George Henry, Scott Zartman, Judith Pope, Elizabeth Brown, Linda Johns, Carol Johnson, Richard Ogden, Jane Roethe, William Huffman, Susan Teubert, Donald Bice, Barbara Dahl, Suzanne Fitzsimmons, Joyce Reilly, Julie Simonson. 3.0 - 3.49 Sandra Anderson, Linda Barrett, Lissa Sherritt, Linda Johnson, Linda Thalacker, Ronald Kanthak, Norma Kopischke, Sandra Kraft, Mary Maves, Phyllis Murwin, Wayne Plautz, Dennis Reppen, Larry Midtbo, Jerel Bieck, Vicki Coplien, Alice Hantke, Jamaeie Meinhardt, Dennis Rosenbaum, Suzanne Wescott, Susan Barron, Joyce Christopherson, Ruth Manson, John Marsden, Marcia Quam, Jeanne Stark, Larry Warkentien, Harley Wredberg, Kenneth Anderson, Esther Cohen, Michael Deems, Jo-Ellen Drogsvold, Larry Fosburgh, Thomas Lenox, Stan Gretebeck, Eunice Kopke. Juniors 4.00 Lisa Falligant, Marie Hubler, David Range, Richard Wagner. 3.5 or above; Terrance Collicott, Patty McGinnity, Marva Maier, Lynne Bartz, Mary Ebbott, Susan Hurd, Susan Hemenway, Roland Carothers, Mary Burns, Kathleen Dickinson, Betty Ford, Judy Anderson, Beth Granzow, Jackie Holgestad Christine Trulson. 3.0 - 3.49; Cynthia Gillette, Cheryl Houfe, Gary Bitter, Mary Davis, Charles Gamble, Gail Lipke, John Spangler, Diane Cohen, Van Sandeen, Darrell Ullius, Fred Falk, Julie Goede, Virginia Moe, Dennis Pratt, Kathryn Roenneburg, Dennis Schwartzlow, Sharon Veitch, Sandy Murwin, Barbara Hull, Dianne Anderson, Robert Brandt, Richard Dray, Thomas Gretebeck, Dianne Halverson, Carol Jenkins, David Johnson, Vicki Kirby, Linda Protteau, Gary Purnell, Sue Sommervold, Patricia Winn. Sophomores, 4.00 Sue Anderson; 3.5 or above, Lynn Paulson, Julie Spike, David Spriggs, Joanne Dietze, Annette McGinnity, Alan Kjernes, Wendy Johnson, Edward Kures, Charles Johnson, Eugene Skrine. 3.00 - 3.49 Eileen Brown, Douglas Dowling, Catherine Ellefson, Philip Manthei, James Raymond, Grace Boxrud, Mary Cedars, Philip Hull, Catherine Rude, Steven Anderson, Dave Bilhorn, Marlin Jung, Theresa McGinnity, Steven Shower, Kathy Deems, Connie Jones Candace Slagg, Catherine Anderson, Dianna Bartz, Marilynn Maves, Wendi Range, Sharon Teisberg, Tom Trumpy.

Back to class. The teen's first quarter of his senior year flew by. Except for stubbing his toe in Mrs. P.'s literature class, he somehow made the first semester honor roll.

With the end of Fall approaching, someone seemed to be speeding up the clock – the clock to uncertainty. Questions still remained like "What are you going to do with your life?"

Once the football season came to a conclusion it was time to sign up for basketball tryouts. Now a senior, it was make the varsity or else. After jumping through the expected hoops, it was a go. He made the varsity roster; so did Joe and Gary. Standing at five feet, seven and a quarter inches, he was walking in the Redwood Forest. It was a very talented team but light on bench strength, however. And, it was the responsibility of the teen and his fellow second stringers to help prepare the big boys for the up-and-coming battles. His new coach, Coach Kemppainen ran well-organized practices, and no opponent was ever taken for granted – conference foe or not.

More on Coach K.

Coach was a slender, athletic guy with his own basketball history originating from Sheboygan Falls High School. About six feet tall, with a blondish-colored flat top, Coach was businesslike in his approach to coaching and teaching. He was not a yeller, at least not much. If he were a ship captain, it would be hard to tell if the waters were calm or stormy – steady as she goes. That is not to say Coach wouldn't get upset. Usually, his dismay was projected by a distinct scowl and wrinkled brow. Sometimes his disapproval was projected by a loud trill of his whistle – "Ok bleacher drill!"

Coach had a very schizophrenic roster. The first five, the starting five, all earned their stripes and gained experience from the previous year's campaign. Understandably, Coach expected a lot from that group, but he didn't let up on the second stringers either. There was work to be done and every athlete, irrespective of talent level was expected to contribute. Coach's preparedness and penchant for planning was noticed by the teen just as sure as the teen was lacing up those white Chuck Taylor Converse All-Stars every practice as well as each and every game. The hours of planning, conditioning, and practicing paid off. The Crimson Tide finished the regular season with a winning record of 18 wins and 7 losses. That wasn't the best part. All of the hours of hard work paid dividends - in spades.

"The" Game

The regular season was in the books. The Wisconsin State Basketball Tournament was under way. Back in the 60's there were no levels or divisions, just the several hundred high schools all competing for the same prize – a trip to the University of Wisconsin Fieldhouse and a date with history.

Coach K.'s Crimson Tide met and defeated their first opponent, conference rival Jefferson. It was nice to get the first one out of the way. Just one problem – the Tide was then slated to face the number two team in the state of Wisconsin, none other than the Monroe Cheesemakers. To make the hill a little steeper, the contest was scheduled to be executed in enemy territory – the Cheesemaker gym. The Cheesemen had yet to lose a game in that gym and were riding high from their coach's 300th win that week. In fact, Monroe had only lost one game to a Freeport, Illinois team and, earlier in the year, beat the eventual state champs, Milwaukee Lincoln.

So, it was a chilly March evening, dressed in their white visitor uniforms, the Tide went through their usual pre-game warm-ups. Coach K. must have had ice water in his veins or all the butterflies in his stomach were flying in formation. When it was all said and done, David slayed Goliath. The second-ranked team in the entire state of Wisconsin had met their match. That talented, senior-laden Edgerton team did it; they did the unexpected. The teen got his proverbial five minutes of fame – OK it was only 30 seconds. When the Tide's starting point guard, Dick Wagner (nka Richard Wagner M.D.) fouled out, Coach K. walked down the bench. The last thing the teen expected was to have his number called. With precious seconds left and a fragile two-point Edgerton lead, the teen nervously entered the game. With one thing on his mind – "Don't screw up – don't foul," the game ended Edgerton 47, Monroe 45. Sophomore Dale Pope scored the winning basket. And so, proudly the boys could return home harboring memories of a lifetime—"The" Game.

We are loyal Edgerton

Loyal and true

Though the odds be great or small

We'll be cheering you, You, rah, rah.

We are loyal Edgerton

True to your name

Fight on to victory

Let's win this game.

As a wonderful postscript, it was over fifty years since the teen, now an old man, had any contact with his coach, Coach K. Thanks to Dr. Wagner, a meeting was scheduled on the teen's familiar turf – the Wisconsin Student Union in Madison. Coach didn't really look much different from his coaching days at Edgerton. Still sporting that sandy-colored crew cut, Coach K. came armed with memorabilia. Of course, pictures and newspaper articles were part and parcel of Coach's historical cache. The two got re-acquainted while perusing the various accounts of how the Crimson Tide pulled off the upset of the 1967 Wisconsin State Basketball Tournament.

Between chatting and reminiscing, Coach issued a heartfelt apology that caused the old man to pause. Coach Kemp apologized for not affording the teen more playing time, more minutes on the court. The old man's reply was without hesitation – simple and straightforward – "I was proud to be a member of that team." The old man, the former player, further amplified. "Coach - you had five players that year, and bluntly speaking, a weak bench, including yours truly. I am proud of you for what you were able to accomplish." In short, "no regrets. I was part of that team".

The visit concluded with a walk through the University of Wisconsin Library Commons. Handshakes were exchanged, hoping it would not be the last time the former player (old man now) talked with his coach. Frankly, the former teen did all he could not get too visibly emotional in front of his coach.

Cagers Shock Monroe, Bow to Vikings

A fired-up Crimson Tide basketball team pulled the upset of the year as they pinned a 47-45 shocker on Monroe, number two ranked team in the state Friday night in W.I.A.A. tourney action but brought the season to a close the following night as they fell to Stoughton 67-42 at Monroe.

The determined Crimson quintet who bowed out with a 15-5 mark, snapped a 15 game Cheesemaker win streak. The Badger Conference champs were undefeated in loop play and were the only club to topple Milwaukee Lincoln, number one in the state.

Heroes were plenty in the big upset but it was the leadership of Dick Pope and the lay-up by brother Dale with 4 seconds remaining that sunk Monroe.

The two teams battled on even terms early and it started out just another ball game as Dale Pope gave the Tide an early 12-7 lead with 6 minutes gone on two quick buckets. Bill Norder, whose 11 points in the first period kept Monroe alive, tossed in 5 but Dick Wagner canned a lay-up and Dick Pope closed out the period with a free toss and two lay-ups; one on a steal and one on a loose ball for a 18-14 Edgerton lead.

In the second quarter it became obvious that the Tide had come to play and really put on a defensive performance. Dick Pope, the game's top point man with 24 points, dropped a rebound with 5 minutes gone but Norder followed with a long swisher. Dale and Wagner followed with two short ones and Dick Holmes, who was a demon on the boards, added a free throw for a 25-16 Crimson lead with two minutes to half time. Holling, who was blanketed by the Tide defense, tipped in a rebound and hit from the circle.

Jeff Lueck got a corner shot before the buzzer and Edgerton led 25-22.

The tempo remained cautious and deliberate in the third period as the Pope brothers traded buckets with Larson and Holling. Dick tallied again from the corner and Dale from medium range and Wagner potted a free throw for a 34-28 margin and the crowd began to sense an upset. Larson tallied a free throw but Dick Pope connected on the buzzer and the Tide held a 36-29 three quarter margin.

Holling, Norder and Larson staged a big comeback drive early in the period but Pope hung in there with 6 free throws and a baseline bucket. Wagner made good on a gift toss for a 45-41 Edgerton lead with 1:30 left. Norder canned a push shot and Larson won a pair of free throws on Wagner's fifth foul to tie it up a 45 all. Larson missed a go ahead opportunity on a free toss with .50 left but the Cheesemakers had obtained possession of the ball and missed a shot with 25 seconds left, Edgerton snared the rebound to set the stage for Dale Pope's winning basket.

The alert Crimson played flawless ball as they pulled off the upset and capitalized on every Cheesemaker mistake. In addition to his offensive show, Dick Pope held Monroe ace, Don Bloom, to zero points. Holman gobbled up 11 big rebounds and held Holling, the 4-year veteran, to 13 points.

Edgerton shot 50% (17-32) from the field and were the better ball club on this evening.

Sixteen fouls were whistled on Monroe while 11 were tooted on Edgerton. Each team missed 8 free throws, Edgerton making 13 and Monroe 11.

Score by quarters:
Edgerton 18-7-11-11-47
Monroe 14-8-7-16- 45

Scoring: Edgerton 17-13-47; Dick Pope 8-8-24; Dale Pope 6-1-13; Holman 0-2-2; and Wagner 3-2-8.
Monroe 17-11-45; Holling 6-1-13; Norder 6-5-17; Larson 4-4-12 and Lueck 1-1-3.

Loss by Monroe Big State 'Upset'

By DENNIS J. SORENSEN
AP Sports Writer

Second-ranked Monroe, the only team to beat mighty Milwaukee Lincoln this season, led the parade of upset victims on the Wisconsin high school basketball tournament trail Friday night.

Erratic Edgerton, beaten twice by Monroe in the regular season, was the team that pulled the 47-45 upset that riddled the Cheesemakers hopes for a second state crown in three years. Monroe, now 17-2, had been undefeated by Wisconsin competition prior to Friday night's upset.

Edgerton, which had finished in the Badger Conference with a 7-3 league record, capped its victory over the highly - rated Cheesemakers when Sophomore Dale Pope notched a short jump shot with four seconds remaining. Dale finished with 13 points and his brother Dick had 24. Edgerton had held a small margin throughout the game until Monroe tied the score at 45 with 55 seconds to play.

All Conference Honors to Pope, Holman

POPE,   HOLMAN

Dick Pope, scrappy Crimson Tide guard and Dick Holman were named to the All Badger Conference team announced this week. Pope was elected for the first team; Holman gained second team selection.

Pope, the top point man for Edgerton this year with 239 markers in loop play, was named to the second team last year. The all-around athlete is gunning for a slam this year as he made the honors in football this fall and is aiming for a repeat in baseball this spring. Pope was also named to all area teams as well as the coveted all-state honors in football.

Holman also is going for the slam as he too was all conference in football and is mound ace of the Crimson baseball team of which he earned honors last season. The durable center was always a scoring threat as he pumped in 203 points and proved to be one of the top rebounders in the loop. His 33 points against Jefferson early in the campaign topped the Crimson individual out put for one game.

Previous players gaining honors in Badger play for Edgerton are: Marty Diegnan 1953-54 and 1954-55, Gary Scharfenberg 1956-57, John Roethe 1959-60 and Stan Edwardson 1965-66.

This year's honor team has: John Selbo - Stoughton - 6-1 Sr.; Ron Schwarz - Middleton - 62 Sr.; Dave Holling - Monroe - 6-5 Sr.; Dick Pope - Edgerton - 5-11 Sr.; Rick Larson - Ft. Atkinson - 5-10 Jr.

The second team has: Mark Polzer - Monona Grove 6-2 Sr.; Gregg Everson - Stoughton - 6-2 Sr.; Dick Holman - Edgerton - 6-4 Sr.; Bill Norder - Monroe - 5-8 Sr.; Dave Harried - Stoughton - 5-8 Sr.

The school days seemed to be passing by with dispatch, too fast as far as the teen was concerned. Seems like he had just gotten there. Now, like his fellow seniors, he was approaching what seemed like a precipice. Next? College probably. If so, which one, what studies? All of those decisions would be sorted out soon, as he was moving quickly through his second semester.

With the basketball season, a satisfying one at that, having concluded, the teen felt a measure of grief. He knew there would be no more basketball games, and no more adrenalin rushes sitting in the locker room receiving last minute instructions from Coach. That was now all in the past. Realistically, aside from making post-graduation decisions, it was just a time to finish his studies and enjoy spending time with his pals. That is just what he did. The basketball season might be over but Rollie's gym was always open. Maybe it was just his imagination, but that winter seemed more daunting than usual. But, in the normal order of things, winter eventually abdicated to spring. With spring sports sign-ups approaching, the teen again debated between baseball or track. As before, track won out because of his buds choosing track. He was OK with that, having finally been awarded the prized "E" – an Edgerton letter for basketball. The teen had no real specialty as far as track went, but he could run some and help out with the relays. So, he thought. It was pure serendipity that the teen unearthed a talent that would propel him to earning another "E".

It was a few days before the first scheduled home track meet. Practice that day was winding down – time to gather up equipment and hit the showers. Heading toward the locker room, the teen had to pass by the broad jump (now long jump) pit. Taking a slight detour, the teen ran down the broad jump runway and executed an impromptu leap. Up in the air and into the pit he went. Curious about the outcome (distance) of his effort, he found a measuring tape that had yet to be retired for the day. Seventeen-plus feet it was. Might just be good enough to persuade Coach Spaeth to enter him in the broad jump for the first meet. Coach raised no objection, and the teen was added to the event, joining fellow jumper Van.

A few days later, the first home meet of the year was underway. As promised, Coach Spaeth entered the teen in the broad jump. When the meet officials called out the teen's name, he positioned himself at the top of the runway. Looking down the skinny cinder-covered path, the pit appeared to be a million miles away. With a stomach full of butterflies, he sprinted toward the white-painted board that defined the legal launch point. The teen felt airborne for an eternity but finally returned to terra firma. Drum roll – the officials stretched out the measuring tape and made the announcement the teen had a leap of over nineteen and a half feet. To boot, he took first place. Edgerton won the event but, more importantly, won their first track meet in years. The teen's fellow jumper, Van took second in the event. His chums Joe and Rollie, racked up points, ensuring a victory for the Crimson Tide thinclads. Not long after his initial surprise leap, the teen was exceeding 20 feet (the "gold" standard) on a regular basis.

The track season went by faster than the teen would have liked. At the outset, the teen had little hope of adding an "E" to compliment his newly acquired varsity basketball letter, but he was awarded another "E" for his track accomplishments, which added an exclamation point to his senior year. A successful campaign with a great group of guys – it didn't get any better. That should be a wrap on the track chapter, but— Rewind for a minute. The teen's satisfaction with his final track season, his final high school athletic competition, was elevated by virtue of an additional unanticipated dividend. At the very outset, the first team meeting, Coach Spaeth made an unusual announcement. Even though Edgerton had yet to form a girl's track team, some of the coeds wanted to practice and work out with the boy's track squad. As Coach went on to explain, the gals could choose any of the available events, and the boys would mentor the ladies accordingly. Kind of unusual back then but it worked out better than expected, at least for one teen.

The teen attended practices, as usual, and found himself mentoring an underclassman, a young lady who showed an interest and a talent as well for the long jump. The teen soon realized how much he looked forward to the end of the school day so he could get to practice (as early as possible). His underling was quiet like himself, but not necessarily shy, more like reserved. Not only was she talented and athletic – she was graceful as a whitetail deer. That was all well and good, but the young lady was also abundantly attractive with dark hair that could have been mistaken for the color of obsidian. With her face adorned with dark brown glasses to match her eyes, there was no other way to put it – the teen was hopelessly smitten with his new understudy.

So now what? The teen is enjoying his role as a mentor, but the young lady is constantly in his thoughts. True to form, the teen was paralyzed by his shyness and engulfed with the fear of hearing "NO" if he was so bold as to ask her out. As always, the teen took the path of least resistance, avoided any risk, and settled for seeing his crush at practices. The final practice was his last encounter with the young beauty. His secret was safe – unrequited love.

Postscript- it was literally the last day of school, and the teen was putting a wrap on his business class (taught by Mr. Spaeth). Coach Spaeth approached the teen and indicated a track scholarship at UW-Whitewater was his for the taking. More on that later.

On To Graduation

With just a few short days to the end of school, the teen's future was rapidly approaching. The recent class trip to Washington, D.C. met all the teen's expectations and more. Damn – Our nation's capital is awesome. And, how in the world those poor teachers kept over a hundred students in line was nothing short of impressive. A remarkable accomplishment at the very least.

Aside from tying up a few loose ends, the only significant business was navigating final exams. Easy enough – sorta. While most teachers elected to require students to complete an exam of some type – usually questions and answers resulting in a final grade, there had to be an exception. Leave it to Mrs. Pavlik, the taskmaster, to assign a term paper in lieu of a final exam. The stated parameters couldn't have been more plain – choose a topic and write X number of words. Simple.

It was the very last day of class for the seniors. Textbooks were being turned in, library fines were reconciled, and last but not least - submit those Pulitzers, Mrs. Pavlik's term papers. Strangely, and much to his teacher's surprise, the teen did not pen an essay as required. One by one the class submitted their compositions – but not the teen. The teen rarely, if ever, bucked authority but he appealed to Mrs. Pavlik to average his grades without the final (term paper), and he would accept whatever grade was appropriate. Unhesitatingly, Mrs. Pavlik would have none of that. She excused herself from the classroom and returned with a handful of sheets of typing paper. She then, quite authoritatively, marched the teen to the typing room and issued the edict, "You're not to leave until I receive your paper". The teen had met his match. It was quiet in the lower level of the building. Most of the students had left by now. Doors to the lockers were conspicuously open as students policed their possessions. The teen came up with a theme and toiled until completion.

What in the world was the kid doing, thinking? The teen explained his feelings in his draft and, once completed as ordered, humbly and respectfully provided Mrs. P. with his last ever high school assignment. In retrospect, the teen was not purposefully being disrespectful to one of his favorite teachers. Rather, he was making a futile and veiled attempt to avoid leaving the nest. It wouldn't have worked anyway. Aside from the out-of-character screwball behavior, one thing was for certain. The slight, diminutive educator was a true pro. She took the challenge head-on and showed volumes of dedication to her craft and recipients. Thank you, Mrs. P.! (Again.)

That was it – no more days left. The final countdown reached zero. Having turned in his last high school assignment, it was time to make his way home. The teen pensively proceeded down that empty hallway toward the office and foyer. It was a walk he had taken hundreds of times, but this was different. It had a different feel – a different purpose. Lacking the usual hustle and bustle, it felt solemn, ponderous. The teen turned left at the front desk and passed through the double doors, marking a change, the magnitude of which the youth had yet to encounter. He was leaving the nest – leaving a place he now felt comfortable calling – HOME.

It seemed like a longer, more sedate walk home that day. The teen felt weighted down by a host of mixed feelings – some comforting like relief but some more nagging, like uncertainty. Even a measure of sadness crept in. For the last time the teen made the walk from Edgerton Community High School up Hwy 59 to the old farmhouse.

Now, it was summer break. Not really a break, more like a developmental line of demarcation. The nagging internal debate about what college to attend was settled. It wasn't really much of a contest. Passing up the track scholarship at UW-Whitewater, the teen decided on the University of Wisconsin–Madison. From the time he could remember, he always wanted to be a Badger. That being said, it was time to find the means to financially support his decision. Jobs were scarce that year and even more scarce for a 17 year-old. With few options to choose from, the teen noticed a job opening in the want ads. He called and was asked to come to work the very next day. The teen hired out on a dairy farm for the Summer. The downside was—he would see little of his buds that Summer, some not for several years.

"Everything is always ending. But everything's always beginning too,"
Patrick Ness

We may never pass this way again—Jim Seals and Dash Crofts

Epilogue

It has been over 60 years since that transplanted teen walked the halls of Edgerton Community High School. Albeit his stay was short, it was a much-needed landing spot. His third high school in three years – he was yearning for some roots. He found them in a place called Edgerton – the community, friends, teachers, and neighbors assisted the youth in finding solid ground. It was Abraham Maslow who coined the phrase "need to belong." And it was exactly what the teen experienced – a sense of belonging.

The former teen's memories of Edgerton are held near to his heart with unwavering fondness. His recollections are as clear as a spring creek. The passage of time has not compromised the clarity of the slide show he harbors in his mind's eye. The mental images of living in a small farming community, nestled in the Rock River valley, are regularly subpoenaed to satisfy the now senior's needs to reminisce. The former teen often finds himself summoning his recollections, many of which appear as postcard-like stills of town, the river, and the old farmhouse. Luckily, the teen back then rarely experienced "There's nothing to do today." Now, for the old man, there is an ample supply of material to satisfy his nostalgic appetite.

Who hasn't said or thought at one time or another, "I wish I could go back…"? Well, what if that teenager could lace up those Converse All-Stars for just one day? Where would he go? What would he do? A trip, on foot, to downtown Edgerton would be obligatory. Maybe just sit out on the front porch watching the traffic go by in hopes that Rollie or Joe might drive up the graveled driveway requesting his presence for another football game or perhaps head to Rollie's for a neighborhood basketball contest.

Without having to think too long, a trip to the woods would be a high priority. Out the back door and a few minutes down a well-worn cow trail was one of the teen's treasured places, a place to enjoy the peace and quiet of the outdoors. Populated by colossal oak and hickory trees, it was an interesting landscape – two very deep bowls that closely mimicked those of the Kettle Moraine. Those two depressions were bisected by a flat, elevated strip of ground about as wide as a driveway – a perfect observation position when stalking the customary prey – gray and fox squirrels, perhaps an occasional cottontail rabbit.

This small parcel, comprised of leaf-bearing hardwoods, was the teen's personal place of quiet and solitude. Worries from the outside world were unwelcomed guests and not allowed entry into the teen's private world. On a warm, sunny fall day, the woods could be as quiet as a crowd listening to a Sunday church sermon. The only intruders, puncturing the silence, emanated from the gentle shimmering of aging leaves. On a good day, the still of the copse would be interrupted by the familiar chattering of squirrels and the cascade of acorns and hickory nuts. The teen's interest was always piqued by the sounds of acorn and hickory nut shells being intercepted by the carpet made by recently fallen leaves. With his trusty companion, his Springfield .22 rifle, hunting was his first priority but soaking up the ambiance was a close second. While the teen immensely enjoyed the pursuit of game, the feeling of well-being he garnered from the outdoors was nothing short of pantheistic. As an added bonus, on some of the warm sunny days, comfortably leaning against a tall oak tree, he could call on the sandman. Then there were those daunting Wisconsin winters back in the 60's. For many, the winter solstice was not eagerly embraced. It just bullishly arrived and forced acceptance of some of Mother Nature's harshest conditions.

Whose woods these are I think I know... Robert Frost
Photo by Dennis Balch

The teen was somewhat ambivalent about this change of season, at least until the first snowfall could be seen from his second story window. Peering out his bedroom window, when it wasn't rendered opaque by the accumulation of frost, the dull looking farm field was no longer a drab khaki hue. The freshly fallen snow blanketed the corn stubble that was the remnant of the fall harvest. For sure, like clockwork, that meant one thing. The teen would predictably be summoned—"Hey Bud—get the hunting jackets out; we're going rabbit hunting". With dispatch, the teen eagerly complied with his father's request. By the time his dad finished his last cup of coffee, the teen had gathered the requisite apparel, as well as those (supposed to be insulated) green rubber boots in preparation for the day's hunt. Cold or not, a walk through the nearby fields and woods was the perfect cure for the winter doldrums. The teen, with his Remington 11-87 over his shoulder and his dad sporting his favorite shooting iron, a Browning A-5, the "contest" was on. Without question the senior could outshoot his offspring, even on a bad day, but the teen was closing in. No matter the outcome of the day, the teen was glad to share his passion for the outdoors with his mentor.

And so, the two would exit the warmth of the farmhouse only to encounter the deceptive elements of a winter day. It was often deceiving—a bluebird day with alluring deep azure skies and unblemished fields appearing to be adorned with a soft layer of cotton. But, hitting the cold air head on generated a personal fog of steamy crystalline clouds with every exhalation.

Each of these iterations with the teen and his dad were memorable, irrespective of the day's harvest. The numbers and tallies have long been forgotten but the former teen, as clear as day, has preserved the mental snap shots of those experiences in toto—priceless.

Although hunting cottontail rabbits was one of the teen's favorite winter pastimes there was some competition for his attentions. Usually, by the time January rolled around, virtually all of the ponds and lakes were ice covered—ice of sufficient thickness to support a myriad of winter sports and activities. And so, the teen would often receive a call from one of his neighbors that lived just down the road. "Hey Chuck—the pond is frozen. Grab your skates and stick. Game (hockey match) starts at noon". After locating those well-worn black leather blades, that were well rested over the course of the warmer months, and donning sufficient warm clothing, the teen was anxiously preparing to make the jaunt down the county road. With skates, stick, and puck in his possession, he walked hurriedly to join his fellow teammates and combatants.

The scene of the competition—it was a small oval shaped body of water, just right for the prized winter event. Tucked away in a grove of tall oak and hickory trees, it was an ideal setting to hold the cold Wisconsin winds in abeyance.

Wasting little time, the teen and his cohorts readied themselves for battle and chose sides. Goals, on each end of the "rink", were crudely constructed and it was time to drop the puck. Hold on—each side needed to designate a goalie or goaltender, if you will. Usually, the least skilled skater (code for not very athletic) drew the short straw and was assigned the job. Almost forgot about the standard rule— "No raising the puck". A rule was implemented to "protect" the poor goalie as he had no protective equipment to mitigate the battering he received from all the incoming pucks.

Hard to say what the fascination was with navigating a rock-hard rubber puck across the frozen surface in 20 below zero weather—maybe it was just being in the outdoors and not the indoors, succumbing to the claustrophobic feeling of being shack happy for days on end. After all, daytime TV was abysmal for most teens—no cable, satellite, or cell phones back in the day. Aside from all that, it was an athletic event and an opportunity to burn off some stored-up energy. And, there was something about the clatter and chatter of steel blades creating a din in an otherwise quiet environment.

The scores and wins of the numerous engagements are all history, forgotten history. The former teen recalls the pristine aesthetics and fellow participants with a decided measure of emotion. It was, without question, Hallmark Christmas card material. Looking back, it almost seems too good to be true, fictional. But, it was indeed real.

And so, the nostalgic ramblings of the septuagenarian (fancy word for old man, senior, et al) have been penned. This essay was authored with a deep sense of gratitude. And, in spite of the passage of time and more than a thousand miles of distance between the author and his buds; phone calls, letters, and social media preserve the relationships. The author is very appreciative of his friends, teammates, and classmates for "keeping the light on".

Sometimes my old school memories sneak out from my eyes and roll down my cheeks... unknown

Jodi, Dan, Chuck with green Rambler

Studying for a test?

Jodi's Birthday with cousins, grandma, Chuck, Dan and Spike -the Labrador

Edgerton's Victory Shocks Cheesemen

Monroe Loses By 47-45 Margin In Meet Opener

Stoughton Faces The Crimson Tide In Finals Tonight

By GARY BABLER

Shocking! That is about the only word to be applied to last evening's regional tournament game as Edgerton slipped past the Monroe Cheesemakers by an unbelievable score of 47-45.

The final blow came on a lay up shot by Dale Pope in the final five seconds. Stoughton took Milton Union, 60 - 45, and will meet Edgerton tonight.

The Cheesemakers never got the customary early lead as the battle seesawed back and forth in the beginning of the game.

Edgerton, however, picked up momentum, and took a 10-6 lead, and Monroe only came as close as within two points of the Crimson Tide before the first quarter ended, 18-14, in favor of Edgerton.

Both teams did very little scoring as the Edgerton style of ball became slow and cumbersome. They built up a nine point edge, and Monroe just couldn't seem to score.

But the Cheesemakers grabbed three quick baskets right before the end of the half to make the score, 25-22. The points came on Dave Holling's two inside shots, and a long archer from Jeff Lueck.

Monroe played basket for basket with Edgerton as they rolled into the third quarter. The Cheesemakers, however, still moved the ball for an inside shot. Edgerton would shift a man down into the middle to play a zone defense to stop the drive shots. Edgerton outscored Monroe 11-7 in the third, and held a 36-29 lead.

Monroe began to chop away at the lead as the fourth period opened. A little at a time, Monroe edged up on Edgerton. First it became 39-34, then 41-38, and 45-43 on a long basket by Bill Norder.

Jim Larson tied the game at 45-45 with a pair of free throws with only 58 seconds remaining.

Monroe then missed a shot with 28 seconds left, and Edgerton grabbed the rebound. Sophomore Dale Pope dropped in a short shot at the 4-second mark for the winning basket.

It took some great spirit on the part of the Cheesemakers to come back in a game where nothing would work for them. Monroe had a lot of trouble trying to get the ball to go in. Time after time shots would not drop in, but sit on the rim, and then fall out.

Bill Norder led the way for Monroe with 17 points. He was followed by Dave Holling at 13, Jim Larson with 12, and Jeff Lueck at 3. Don Bloom didn't score, but did well on the boards.

The Cheesemakers compiled a very fine 17-2 record this season, with this defeat being their first loss in the state of Wisconsin.

Holling, Norder, Lueck, Mark Winzenried, Daryle Wilde, and Gary Babler are all senior members on the team, and have played four fine years of basketball with the Cheesemakers.

It was a heartbreaker for the whole team, coach Mitchell, and his staff. Last week, Mitchell won his 300th game, and deserves that and more for his tremendous job of coaching at Monroe.

Dennis Balch, Joe Peterson, Gary Purnell, Jim Rynning, Dick Wagner, Dan Bice, Coach Tom Kemppainen, Chuck Gamble, Dick Pope, Dale Pope, Les Nickel, Dick Holman, George Sherman.

Edgerton Crimson Tide 1967

Rich, Chuck, Terry, Rollie, Rollie's bro Dennis, Gary

"Ain't it good to know you have a friend," James Taylor

Acknowledgement

As with any major endeavor in life, there are usually a number of individuals that contribute to a successful conclusion. This project was no exception. The author would like to thank the following individuals for their reviews and comments: Joe, Rollie, Terry, Sandy, Julie, Nancy, Janet, Mary, Dick (3), Dennis, Gary, and Ted.

Thanks to my mentors, teachers, and coaches, especially Coach K. for providing pictures and news clips.

About the Author

The author was born and raised in southern Wisconsin. After graduating high school (Edgerton, Wis), he attended the University of Wisconsin-Madison and completed his BA in 1971. His love of the outdoors lured him "Out West," where he met his wife, Katherine. Except for a brief stint in Tennessee to finish his doctorate, he has largely lived in Idaho. He is now retired and lives in the mountains of northern Idaho, Hells Gulch specifically, with Katherine and their loyal Labrador companions, Libby and Hank.

www.ingramcontent.com/pod-product-compliance
Lightning Source LLC
Chambersburg PA
CBHW052207110526
44591CB00012B/2114